THE ALAMO

AMERICAN SYMBOLS

Lynda Sorensen

The Rourke Book Company, Inc.
Vero Beach, Florida 32964

PHOTO CREDITS
© James P. Rowan: cover, pages 7, 12, 13, 21; © Frank Balthis:
title page, page 18; courtesy Daughters of the Republic of Texas
Library at the Alamo: pages 4, 8, 10, 15, 17

Library of Congress Cataloging-in-Publication Data

Sorensen, Lynda, 1953–
    The Alamo / by Lynda Sorensen
        p. cm. — (American symbols)
    Includes index
    ISBN 1-55916-049-7
    1. Alamo (San Antonio, Tex.)—Juvenile literature.
    [1. Alamo (San Antonio, Tex.) 2. National monuments]
    I. Title II. Series.
    F390.S697 1994
    976.4'351—dc20   94–7054
                                                  CIP
                                                  AC

Printed in the USA

TABLE OF CONTENTS

THE ALAMO

The Alamo has long been remembered for the courage and **heroism** of the men who fought there.

The Alamo was an old Spanish **mission** that became a bloody battleground in San Antonio, Texas.

A stubborn force of Texans and Americans held off Mexican General Antonio Lopez de Santa Anna's huge army for 12 days.

Finally, on March 6, 1836, Mexican soldiers poured over the Alamo's stone walls. The defenders were wiped out. The Alamo's fall became a lasting **symbol** of American bravery.

Lt. Colonel William Travis rallied his small force of Texans behind the Alamo walls

SAN ANTONIO DE VALERO

Spanish Catholic priests built the original Alamo in 1718. It was named San Antonio de Valero, later becoming the Alamo.

San Antonio de Valero was much like other Spanish missions. It had rooms, buildings and a **plaza**, or open area, surrounded by tall, thick walls.

In those days Spain controlled Mexico. Texas and much of the American Southwest were then part of Mexico.

Priests used the missions as churches and schools for peaceful Indians. The walls kept warlike Indians away.

Little except the church (shown here) remains of the original San Antonio de Valero

RUMBLINGS OF WAR

The population of Texas underwent changes in the early 1800's. Americans began to settle among the native Mexicans. The newcomers soon outnumbered the Mexicans.

Meanwhile, in 1821, Mexico won independence from Spain. Texas was now Mexican property.

General Santa Anna became the president and **dictator** of Mexico in 1833. Texans of both Mexican and American backgrounds were angered by Santa Anna's harsh rule.

Many Texans wanted Texas to be a free nation. Texans formed an army and attacked Mexican soldiers.

Theodore Gentilz' drawing of the Alamo's fall was begun in the 1840's and probably completed in the 1880's

RETREAT TO THE ALAMO

Santa Anna was furious. He moved quickly to crush the **revolution**, or uprising, against him. He marched with an army of about 2,500 men to San Antonio in February, 1836.

There an "army" of some 150 Texans was led by 26-year old Lieutenant Colonel William Travis. Travis and his little band retreated behind the Alamo's walls.

On March 3, 1836, Col. Travis told his men: "There is still time to escape! Let those who choose to stay and die with me step across this line."

A monument stands where Santa Anna defeated Col. Fannin's army two weeks after the Alamo at the Battle of Coleto

Santa Anna took 400 Texan prisoners from the battle and shot them here at Goliad

UNDER ATTACK

The Texans could have scattered. They did not have to stand up to the Mexican army. Even after they entered the Alamo, the men had chances to slip away. But only one man did.

Santa Anna told Travis that he would kill every man in the Alamo. Travis said he would never surrender.

Travis hoped to get help from either General Sam Houston or Colonel James Fannin. Fannin refused, and Houston was too far away.

On February 23 the Mexicans began firing cannon shells at the Alamo.

The Alamo lay in ruins after the Mexican attack in March, 1836

THE FINAL ATTACK

Little happened for nearly two weeks. In time Santa Anna could have destroyed the Alamo with cannons. Instead, he foolishly ordered an attack by his foot soldiers on March 6.

The Mexican soldiers were no less brave than the Texans. For an hour they were mowed down as they charged the Alamo walls.

Mexican soldiers finally crossed over the Alamo walls by climbing ladders.

This artist's view of the crumbling Alamo was printed in 1851 in Grahams Magazine

THE LAST FIGHT

The battle raged inside the Alamo walls. Gunfire, screams and shouts were deafening. Soon out of bullets, the badly outnumbered Texans fought with clubs and rifle butts. The fighting ended quickly.

Santa Anna spared the lives of a slave and nine women and children. Travis and his entire force of 189 men were killed. Among the dead were several Texans of Mexican background and two famous men of the American frontier—Davey Crockett and Jim Bowie.

A hotel named for the most famous of Alamo defenders rises above the Alamo church

"REMEMBER THE ALAMO!"

Santa Anna turned his army toward Sam Houston. But General Houston kept a step ahead. His army of Texans grew larger each day as the story of the Alamo spread.

On April 21 the Texans suddenly turned and surprised the Mexican army. With cries of "Remember the Alamo!" the Texans killed 630 Mexican soldiers at San Jacinto, Texas, in an 18-minute battle.

Santa Anna was captured, and in May, Mexico granted freedom to Texas. In 1845 the free Republic of Texas joined the United States.

Goliad State Historical Park's marker recalls the Battle of Coleto and Col. Fannin's defeat

BATTLE OF COLETO
AND
GOLIAD MASSACRE

AFTER THE FALL OF THE ALAMO, MARCH 6, 1836, COLONEL JAMES WALKER FANNIN, WITH ABOUT 400 SOLDIERS, MOSTLY VOLUNTEERS FROM THE UNITED STATES IN THE TEXAS WAR FOR INDEPENDENCE, WAS ORDERED BY TEXAS GENERAL SAM HOUSTON TO RETREAT FROM GOLIAD TO VICTORIA.

MARCH 19, THE HEAVY MEXICAN FORCE OF GENERAL URREA SURROUNDED THE WITHDRAWING TEXAS CONTINGENT NEAR COLETO CREEK, AND BITTER FIGHTING ENSUED. FANNIN'S VOLUNTEERS HURLED BACK THE ASSAULTS OF THE MEXICAN FORCE. ON THE FOLLOWING DAY, FACED WITH SEVERAL TIMES THEIR NUMBER, THE TEXANS SURRENDERED IN THE BELIEF THEY WOULD BE TREATED AS PRISONERS OF WAR OF A CIVILIZED NATION. AFTER REMOVAL TO GOLIAD, THE FANNIN MEN WERE MARCHED OUT AND MASSACRED ON PALM SUNDAY UNDER ORDERS OF SANTA ANNA, THE GENERAL OF THE MEXICAN ARMIES. THUS DICTATOR SANTA ANNA ADDED ANOTHER INFAMY TO THAT OF THE ALAMO AND GAVE TO THE MEN WHO SAVED TEXAS AT SAN JACINTO THEIR BATTLE CRY, "REMEMBER THE ALAMO, REMEMBER GOLIAD".

THE MEMORIAL TO FANNIN AND HIS MEN IS NEAR GOLIAD.

(1974)

VISITING THE ALAMO

The original buildings and walls of the Alamo largely disappeared through misuse. Today's "Alamo" is actually the original chapel and a **re-creation**, or copy, of the old mission.

The four-acre Alamo is owned by the state of Texas. The grounds are a national historic landmark, a place of honor. The Alamo is operated by the Daughters of the Republic of Texas.

Americans and Mexicans alike remember the Alamo and the spirit of the brave men who fought there.

Glossary

dictator (DIHK tay ter) — someone who rules with little or no direction from other people

heroism (HEHR o izm) — great courage

mission (MIH shun) — a small, walled village where Spanish Catholic priests set up schools and churches for Indians in the 16th, 17th and 18th centuries

plaza (PLAH zuh) — square or rectangular open area within a town or mission

re-creation (RE kree A shun) — a place or building that has been built to look like an earlier place or building

revolution (REH vo lu shun) — an uprising by people against their own government; a revolt

symbol (SIM bull) — something which stands for something else, as a flag stands for a country

INDEX